The Girl Who Could Sing with the Birds

An Inspirational Tale
about Rachel Carson

The Girl Who Could Sing with the Birds

Maya Cointreau

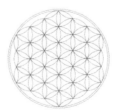

An Earth Lodge® Publication
www.earthlodgebooks.com
Roxbury, Connecticut

Copyright 2015 by Maya Cointreau
Printed & Published in the United States by Earth Lodge®

ISBN 978-1514296295

All Artwork, Layout & Design by Maya Cointreau

"Those who contemplate the beauty of the earth find reserves of strength that will endure as long as life lasts. There is something infinitely healing in the repeated refrains of nature - the assurance that dawn comes after night, and spring after winter."

Rachel Carson

Deep in the forest

    wading through streams

    young Rachel Carson

    explored as she dreamed.

Her home on a farm

was a broad wonderland

filled with creatures of nature

she could touch with her hands.

Between wild ramblings

and time spent at school,

her mother taught Rachel

that Nature was cool.

As she grew she explored

the sands by the sea

discovering wonders

in the waters beneath.

Rachel wanted to share

   all the things that she saw

   and started to write

   her own stories of awe.

But how did we work?

How did we grow?

These were the things

she still wanted to know.

Life thrived all around,

in the ocean and trees,

inspiring Rachel to study

the science of we.

Writing was happy work.

Science filled her brain.

Combining the two

felt right as rain.

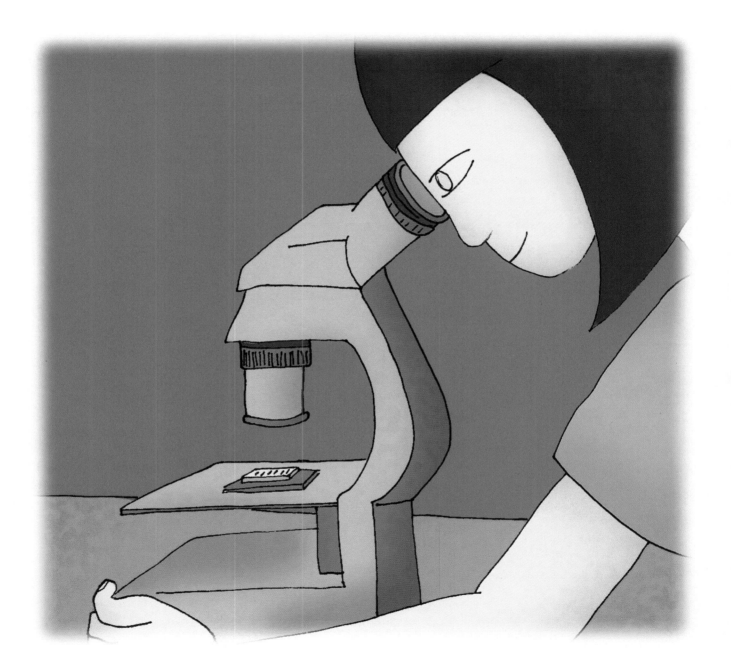

She loved the earth,

the beach and zoology.

She put it all together

with marine biology.

She talked on the radio

about the oceans around us

teaching all fishes

really are precious.

Rachel worried about pollution,

fish, birds and flowers.

Would nature's song

go on for years, or just hours?

Science was brilliant,

it could change the whole world,

but we had to be careful

how plans were unfurled.

When we use chemicals

to control Mother Nature

we might hurt bees and birds,

or poison our acres.

What we do to the planet

we do to ourselves.

Poisons have no place in fields

or on kitchen shelves.

Rachel wrote many books,

and started a movement,

people caring about life

and nature's improvement.

Earth Day was founded

so now we all know,

the world is a special place

where good things can grow.

More About Rachel

Rachel Louise Carson was born on her family farm in Pennsylvania on May 27th in 1907. She spent her formative years developing a strong love of nature. She studied literature and marine biology at Chatham University (then known as the Pennsylvania College for Women), followed by marine biology at the Marine Biological Laboratory and zoology and genetics at Johns Hopkins. She worked as an aquatic biologist and educational writer with the US Fish and Wildlife services and wrote several books urging the preservation of our oceans and planet.

During her research, Carson became increasingly worried about the environmental effects of pesticides and chemicals such as DDT. Her book *Silent Spring*, which linked the overuse of pesticides with bird deaths and environmental degradation, is credited by many as having given rise to the environmental movement of the 60s, birthing the Environmental Protection Agency and Earth Day. She spent the latter part of her life focusing on conservationism and often explained that one of the most important things we can pass on to our children is a love and understanding of nature.

"If a child is to keep alive his inborn sense of wonder, he needs the companionship of at least one adult who can share it, rediscovering with him the joy, excitement, and mystery of the world we live in," Carson reminded parents.

"A child's world is fresh and new and beautiful, full or wonder and excitement," believed Carson. "It is our misfortune that for most of us that clear-eyed vision, that true instinct for what is beautiful and awe-inspiring, is dimmed and even lost before we reach adulthood. If I had influence with the good fairy who is supposed to preside over the christening of all children, I should ask that her gift to each child in the world be a sense of wonder so indestructible that it would last throughout life, as an unfailing antidote against the boredom and disenchantment of later years… the alienation from the sources of our strength."

Carson died on April 14th, 1964, and was awarded the Presidential Medal of Freedom for Environmentalism by Jimmy Carter in 1980.

Photo courtesy of United States Fish and Wildlife Service

Biographical and Quotation sources: Rachelcarson.org, Famousscientists.org, US Fish and Wildlife Service, The Independent, Wikipedia and Carson's books *Silent Spring* and *The Sense of Wonder*.

About the Author

Maya Cointreau has been writing and drawing all her life. She lives on a farm in Connecticut with her family, a pack of poodles, a herd of horses, a flock of chickens, and a cartload of cats. For more information about her other books and CDs, visit her website at http://www.mayacointreau.com.